Why Does the Moon Change Its Shape?

Patricia J. Murphy

The Rosen Publishing Group's
PowerKids Press™
New York

To my "far out" family!

Published in 2004 by The Rosen Publishing Group, Inc.
29 East 21st Street, New York, NY 10010

First Edition

Editor: Frances E. Ruffin
Book Design: Danielle Primiceri
Layout: Michael de Guzman

Photo Credits: Cover © Mark Stephensen/CORBIS; pp. 4, 8 top © Digital Vision; pp. 7, 8 bottom, 15, 19 © Photri-Microstock; pp. 11, 16 © PhotoDisc; p. 12, 20 © Roger Ressmeyer/CORBIS.

Murphy, Patricia J., 1963–
Why does the moon change its shape? / by Patricia J. Murphy.— 1st ed.
    p. cm. — (The library of why)
Includes bibliographical references and index.
ISBN 0-8239-6234-2 (library binding)
1. Moon—Miscellanea—Juvenile literature. [1. Moon.] I. Title. II. Library of why?
QB582 .M87 2003
523.3—dc21
                                        2001005466

Manufactured in the United States of America

Contents

What Is the Moon?

The night sky would not be the same without the changing face of the Moon. The Moon is Earth's only natural **satellite**. This ball of rock **orbits**, or circles, Earth at 2,300 miles per hour (3,701 km/h). It is one-fourth of the size of Earth. It measures 2,160 miles (3,476 km) across and 6,800 miles (10,943 km) around. Moon rocks brought back by astronauts reveal that the Moon is made of rock, including basalt and other **minerals**. Below the Moon's thick crust are its mantle, or middle layer, and its liquid center, or core.

◀ *The Moon is Earth's closest neighbor. It is only 238,857 miles (384,403 km) away. The Moon may be 4.6 billion years old.*

How Was the Moon Formed?

Throughout the years, scientists have had different ideas about how the Moon was formed. One idea was that Earth and the Moon were once parts of a planet that was still forming. As the planet spun, part of it pulled away and became the Moon. After scientists studied moon rocks brought back by astronauts, many believed that a small planet had crashed into Earth. Pieces of Earth's outer layer broke off and formed the Moon. This might explain why Earth and the Moon share some of the same **matter**.

This is a close-up photograph of the near side of the Moon. ▶

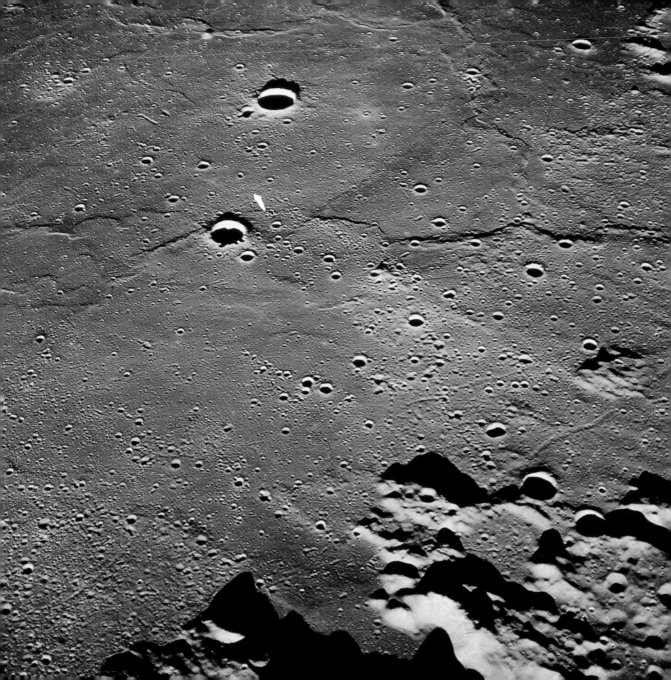

Near Side of the Moon ◄

◄ **Far Side of the Moon**

How Does the Moon Get Around?

The Moon completes a single **revolution** around Earth every 27 days and 8 hours. Earth's **gravity** keeps the Moon in Earth's orbit. The Moon has gravity, too. It is only one-sixth the strength of Earth's gravity. Something that weighs 300 pounds (136 kg) on Earth would weigh only 50 pounds (23 kg) on the Moon. The Moon also spins on its **axis** as it orbits Earth. We always see the same side of the Moon. This side is called the near side. The other side is the far side of the Moon. Only astronauts have seen the far side close up.

◄ *We see only the near side of the Moon from Earth. Our gravity causes it to spin on its axis at about the same speed as Earth.*

What Are the Phases of the Moon?

As the Moon revolves around Earth, it appears to change its shape. What really changes is the Moon's position in relation to the Sun and Earth. For example, the moon appears dark when it is between Earth and the Sun. These changes are called **lunar phases**. Each phase is like a picture postcard from the Moon. It tells us where the Moon is on its trip around Earth. A half-moon shows that it is one-quarter of the way around Earth. A full moon shows that it is half of the way around. The opposite page shows phases of the Moon.

These photos show phases of the Moon. The Moon is said to wax as it appears to grow and to wane as it appears to shrink. ▶

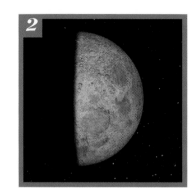

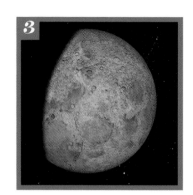

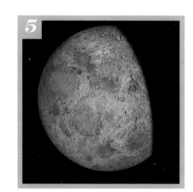

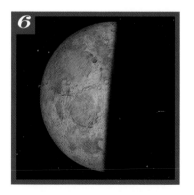

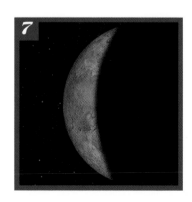

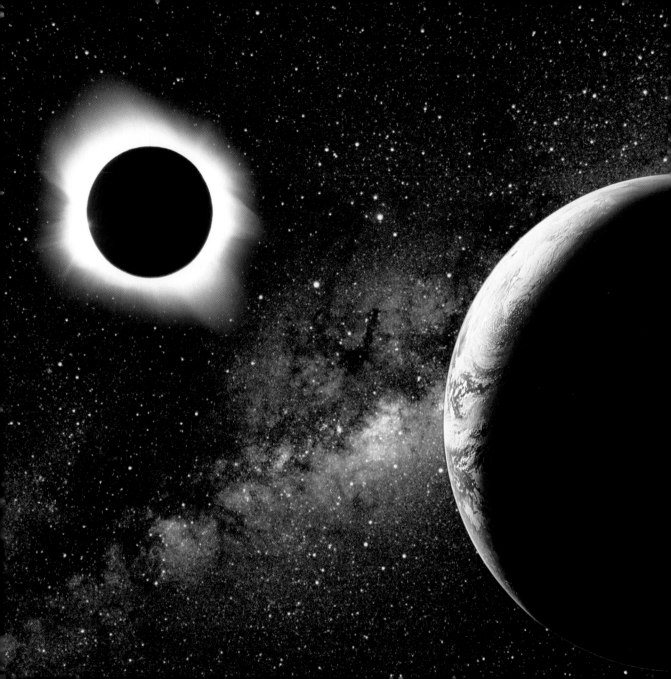

What Makes a Lunar Eclipse?

A lunar eclipse occurs when the Sun, Earth, and the Moon line up. During this event, Earth's orbit passes between the Sun and the Moon. Earth casts a shadow on the Moon and blocks the sunlight that lights the Moon. Long ago, people couldn't explain events like lunar eclipses. Some people thought the moon had special powers. Some even worshiped the Moon. Others believed that it made rain fall and crops grow. Many used the Moon to keep track of good months to farm. The sky was Earth's first calendar!

◀ *Lunar eclipses can be seen somewhere on Earth two to three times each year.*

How Does the Moon Cause Tides?

The Moon's gravity pulls on Earth. Earth feels these pulls in its waters. The pulls cause tides, which are rises and falls of water in the sea and in other large bodies of water. Waters facing the Moon have high tides. Waters on the other side of Earth, farther away from the Moon, are low and weak. Tides follow the Moon's orbit. When there is a high tide in one place, there is a low tide in the opposite place on Earth. People who sail or fish need high tides to prevent their boats from hitting rocks or from getting stuck on a sandy bottom.

This is a picture of the sea at high tide. All around the world, tides rise and fall every 12 hours and 26 minutes. ▶

Is There Life on the Moon?

There is no **atmosphere** on the Moon. This means that there is no air, wind, weather, or water. Without these things, nothing can grow. The lack of atmosphere cannot protect the Moon from the Sun's heat by day or hold onto heat at night. During the daytime on the Moon, its **temperatures** can reach 225°F (107°C). At night the Moon's temperature can drop to -243°F (-153°C). Because there is no wind or rain on the Moon, its surface has not changed in millions of years!

◄ *The Moon's surface is covered with dust, dark flatlands, huge pothole-like craters, and mountains.*

Who First Walked on the Moon?

On July 20, 1969, astronaut Neil Armstrong took the first human step on the Moon. His footprint is still there! From 1969 through 1972, 12 U.S. astronauts walked on the Moon. They brought back moon rocks and soil to study. Since 1972, there have been no manned flights to the Moon. In 1998, the National Aeronautics and Space Administration (NASA) launched the *Lunar Prospector*, a spacecraft built to explore the Moon. On board was a **probe** that collected information about the Moon.

In 1969, astronauts Neil Armstrong and Edwin "Buzz" Aldrin spent 2 hours and 21 minutes on the surface of the Moon. ▶

Could We Ever Live on the Moon?

Someday people may call the Moon home. People might be able to live in a space station on the Moon. This station would have air for people to breathe and food for them to eat. It would also protect them from the cold and the heat. People would also need water. NASA's *Lunar Prospector* probe discovered ice on the Moon's North and South Poles. Scientists believe this ice comes from **comets**. The ice could be used to make water, oxygen, and fuel.

◀ *This photo shows a NASA spaceship and the Moon. One day travelers might stop off at the Moon, then go on to other planets.*

How Can We Best Observe the Moon?

Moon watching can be far out and fun! Here are a few suggestions for moon watching. Choose a safe spot for viewing. If it is away from your home, ask an adult to join you. Bring along a pair of **binoculars** or a telescope. Carry a flashlight to help you see in the dark. Keep a moon-watching journal. Write down the date, the time, and the place each time that you moon watch. Draw the Moon's phases. Join or start an astronomy club. Keep your eyes on the skies. You never know what you'll see!

Glossary

atmosphere (AT-muh-sfeer) The layers of gases, or air, that surround Earth.

axis (AK-sis) An imaginary line that passes through the middle of a planet.

binoculars (buh-NAH-kyuh-lurz) A small telescope that enables distant things to appear close, and small things large.

comets (KAH-mits) Bright bodies of ice and dust that have tails.

gravity (GRA-vih-tee) The force that keeps objects down.

lunar phases (LOO-nur FAY-zez) The stages of the Moon as seen from Earth.

matter (MA-tur) A solid, liquid or gas that has weight and takes up space.

minerals (MIN-rulz) Natural ingredients from Earth's soil, such as coal or copper, that are not plants or animals.

orbits (OR-bits) Circular paths traveled by planets around the Sun.

probe (PROHB) An instrument that is used to study space.

revolution (reh-vuh-LOO-shun) A path taken by a planet or the Sun.

satellite (SA-til-eyt) An object that travels around a larger body.

temperatures (TEM-pruh-cherz) How hot or cold something is.

Index

A
Armstrong, Neil,
    18
astronaut(s), 6, 18

C
core, 5
crust, 5

E
Earth, 5–6, 9,
    13–14

G
gravity, 9, 14

L
lunar eclipse, 13
lunar phases, 10
Lunar Prospector,
    18, 21

M
mantle, 5
matter, 6
moon rocks, 5–6,
    18

N
NASA, 18, 21

S
satellite, 5
Sun, 13, 17

T
tides, 14

Web Sites

Due to the changing nature of Internet links, PowerKids Press has developed an online list of Web sites related to the subject of this book. This site is updated regularly. Please use this link to access the list:
www.powerkidslinks.com/low/moonchg/